Mirror Mirror...
Am I Beautiful?
Leader's Guide

Looking Deeper to Find Your True Beauty
With Shelley Hitz, Heather Hart, & Michelle Neff

This book is designed to be used with *Mirror Mirror... Am I Beautiful?* 2nd Edition.

Mirror Mirror... Am I Beautiful? Leader's Guide
Looking Deeper to Find Your True Beauty

Written by Shelley Hitz and Heather Hart
with Michelle Neff

Copyright © 2009, 2016 Shelley Hitz and Heather Hart

Published by Body and Soul Publishing
   P.O. Box 6542
   Colorado Springs, CO 80934

All rights reserved. No part of this publication may be reproduced, stored in a retrieval system, or transmitted by any means – electronic, mechanical, photographic (photocopying), recording, or otherwise – without prior permission in writing from the author, unless it is for the furtherance of the Gospel of salvation and given away free of charge.

1st edition cover design by Megan Six
2nd edition cover updated by Heather Hart

Cover graphic © eurobanks – stock.adobe.com
Chapter art © evegenesis and Africa Studio – stock.adobe.com

Printed in the United States of America

ISBN-10: 1-946118-02-8
ISBN-13: 978-1-946118-02-8

All scripture quotations, unless otherwise indicated, are taken from the Holy Bible, New International Version® 1973, 1978, 1984 by International Bible Society. Used by permission of Zondervan Publishing House. All rights reserved.

CONTENTS

Note to Leaders 1
Session 1: The Pretty Problem 7
Session 2: Subliminal Beauty Messages 11
Session 3: Beauty Lies 15
Session 4: What Do You Believe? 19
Session 5: Faith & Fashion 23
Session 6: Modest is Hottest 27
Session 7: Boy Crazy 31
Session 8: Guys vs. Girls 35
Session 9: When Sex Isn't Sexy 39
Session 10: Find Your True Beauty 43
Session 11: The Beauty of Hope 47
Session 12: You Are Beautiful 51

Note to Leaders

Thank you so much for volunteering to lead a study through our book, *Mirror Mirror... Am I Beautiful?* We so appreciate you! For years God has been using this study in the lives of teen girls around the globe, and we know He will use it in the lives of the teen girls in your life.

Before we get started we want to let you know what to expect from this study. Each session has some tips for leader preparation and then an outline for the study session. As the leader, we highly recommend reading the whole book before the study starts, and then reading it again with the girls. That way you know what to expect.

On that note, this is the leaders guide, and you will need a copy of our book as well. As will each girl who is going through this study with you. You can download the PDF free from our website, or purchase copies online from TrueBeautyBook.com. All of the resources that are available on our website are free for you to reprint as needed. We just ask that you don't distribute them online or remove any copyright information.

Each of the girls books will have the Bible study guide in the back, however if you would rather print out the questions for them, handouts are available on our website at handouts.TrueBeautyBook.com. This is especially helpful for girls using the PDF of the book, or a Kindle copy.

For each session, girls will need to bring their book, Bible, a pen or pencil, and their journal. If you are providing journals, you will pass them out at the first session. If you are not, make sure girls know to pick one up ahead of time.

We also recommend that you create a playlist with soft music to use during the reflection times. We highly recommend instrumental music so the girls don't get too focused on listening to the words or singing along.

Quick Tips for Successful Bible Study

We also want to share just a few quick tips to help you and your girls get the most out of this study.

- Encourage girls to read the book each week, but don't let them get too discouraged if they couldn't. They will still get a ton out of this study just by being in the group.
- Teens love snacks. You don't have to feed them a meal, but if you can have soda and some munchies, the girls will be thrilled.
- Try to draw out quiet teens and get them involved, but don't embarrass them.
- Make sure you speak to each girl individually at least once each meeting.
- Do your best to visit with at least one girl each week outside of the session (this could be on social media or in person).
- Pray for your girls. Pray hard. Being a teen girl in today's world is **hard**. They need more prayer than you could ever imagine.
- Be a good example. Many girls today do not have a godly role model they can look up to, and by leading this study, you could inadvertently become it. Do your best to love each girl the way God loves them and to display true beauty. But also be willing to admit that you still struggle too.
- Consider getting blank cards to send to the girls who attended your study. You can send out a couple each week letting the girls know why you appreciate them. You can find some of our designs at cards.TrueBeautyBook.com.

Thanks again for investing in the lives of today's teen girls. If you have any questions or comments for us, you can find our contact information in the back of this book.

Bible Study Leader's Guide

For Group Study

Session One

The Pretty Problem
Chapters 1, 2 & 3

Leader Preparation

Pray that God would help you to be content with the girls who show up. No matter who is there or not there, whether the number is big or small, ask that He equips you to be the leader they need.

Set up a television or computer to watch the video to open this lesson. You can have the video ready to go by pulling it up on our website, or by searching for it on YouTube.

Consider looking at the responses girls have submitted at http://www.teen-beauty-tips.com/advertising-and-body-image.html and choosing one or two thoughts from there to share with the girls.

Print handouts if you plan to use them.

Supplies
- TV and internet access (to watch the video)
- A Notebook for each girl*
- Arts and Crafts supplies to decorate journals (glue, markers, stickers, cardstock, etc.)
- Whiteboard

* You can get cheap notebooks or even composition notebooks for the girls to decorate. If you don't have a budget, ask each girl to bring their own (but maybe have a few on hand just in case someone forgets). You may also want to decorate your own journal in advance to use as an example.

Group Study

Introduction

Welcome girls as they come in and let them know you are glad they came. Also let them know where they can sit and any other instructions that might be specific to your group.

Once everyone has arrived, introduce the study and yourself, then go around the room and have each girl say their name, school, grade, and maybe something they like to do in their free time.

Pray

Open your session by thanking God for each girl that came and praying that He would use your time together for His glory.

Opening Activity

Watch the Evolution commercial as a group.

After the video, point out the Share Your Thoughts section at the end of chapter one in the book. Ask them if they think it's fair for the media to portray such an unrealistic "perfect image" for how we should look, and if it impacts our self-esteem and body image.

Remind them that they can share their thoughts online, or even log on to see what other girls are saying. Share any thoughts you found on the website from other girls, or here's what Miranda shared:

> "When I look at magazines or TV or whatever, all I see is what I'm not. I have dark wavy hair and milk chocolate eyes with a tint if gold in them. I am tall and average weight and am so sick of the media airbrushing models and making me see what I'm not. I've been told I'm pretty, but I have trouble

believing it. I'm not blonde haired, blue-eyed, confident and flirty. When the media showcases these qualities, I notice everything I'm not. I never feel pretty and I believe a big part of that is because of the media."

Discuss

Each of the girls should have the following questions in the back of their books. Have them get their books out and flip there now, or if you have printed handouts, you can pass those out now.

Note: Even if you are using handouts, the girls should still have their books to use for reference when answering the questions.

Ask if each of the girls had a chance to read the first three chapters. If not, let them know that's okay, and recommend they read them before the next session. Then proceed with the questions for this session.

1. Who or what do you think influences you the most on your ideas of what it means to be beautiful?

2. Do you believe you were created to be beautiful? Why or why not?

3. How do you think God would define "beautiful"? What makes us beautiful in His eyes? *(Leader note: Write their answers on a whiteboard.)*

4. *Have someone read Ambers story in chapter 3.* Can anyone relate to Amber's story? If so, in what ways?

5. If someone came to you with a similar problem, what encouragement would you offer them?

6. *Look up Colossians 3:23-24 and have someone read it aloud.* What can we learn about beauty from those verses?

Reflection

Encourage girls to think about this question: What is one thing you could do this week to focus more on your inner beauty instead of just your outer beauty? Invite them to share, or just silently consider it.

Prayer Time

Ask girls if they have any prayer requests they would like to share. Say a prayer asking God to use this study in the lives of each girl who is there. Ask that He would help them focus on their true beauty.

Fun Activity

Decorate journals to use during the study. Remind the girls to make them pretty inside and out.

Before You Dismiss

Remind girls when your next meeting is and that they should:
- Read Psalm 139 and write a prayer thanking God for the way He created them in their journal.
- Read Chapters 4 & 5.

Also
- Invite them to bring their favorite Barbie or other type of doll from when they were younger to the next session.
- Let the girls know that you are available to talk with them one on one. If you are comfortable doing so, make sure they have your contact information. You might even consider creating a private Facebook group for your study group.

Session Two

Subliminal Beauty Messages
Chapters 4 & 5

Leader Preparation

Pray that God would help you to be content with the girls who show up. No matter who is there or not there, whether the number is big or small, ask that He equips you to be the leader they need and perceptive of their needs.

Set up the location of your study so everyone will be comfortable and feel like part of the group. Also, set up to play soft music during the reflection time. You may want to prepare a playlist specifically for this time.

Consider bringing your own doll or if you are a mom, one of your children's dolls to share with them.

Print handouts if needed.

Group Study

Introduction

Welcome all the girls as they come in and note any new attendees. If needed, make introductions once everyone is seated.

Pray

Invite the Holy Spirit to guide your discussion and open your hearts to His truth.

Review

Ask if anyone was able to do something this week to focus more on their inner beauty than on their outer beauty.

Ask if anyone wants to share something they read about from the past two chapters and how it impacted them.

Discuss

Pass out handouts or have girls flip to the questions in the back of their books, then discuss the questions.

1. What did you think about the story of Cindy Jackson trying to become Barbie?

2. What about you? What influences in your life have shaped the way you view your body (internet/magazines/television shows)? Is there a media that may be influencing you indirectly, such as Heather shared about near the end of chapter 4?

3. Share about the doll you brought, or if you don't have one, share about your favorite doll from when you were younger

and how you think it might have influenced your body image.

4. What would be some signs that you might be addicted to social media? (Could you be addicted?)

5. Do you think there is any danger in portraying a false image of yourself on social media?

6. Does what we post on social media really matter? Why or why not?

After you have answered that question, have someone read Matthew 7:15-20 aloud. Ask: Did your answer change?

Reflection

Have someone read the six questions at the end of chapter five (three from Mandy J. Hoffman's book, and the three Heather and Shelley added). Give the girls some quiet time (or play some soft music in the background) and have them answer these questions in their journal (or on a piece of paper). Encourage them to ask God to reveal to them any changes they may need to make.

Prayer Time

Ask if the girls have any prayer requests. Close in prayer, mentioning any requests they had and praying for God to help open their eyes in the area of beauty and help them to see themselves the way that He sees them.

Before You Dismiss

Remind girls when your next meeting is and that they should:
- Journal about how media (of any kind) has been influencing their self-image.
- Read Chapters 6 & 7 for the next session.

Also, remind the girls that you are available to talk with them one on one.

Session Three

Beauty Lies
Chapters 6 & 7

Leader Preparation

Pray that God would help you to be content with the girls who show up. No matter who is there or not there, whether the number is big or small, ask that He equips you to be the leader they need and perceptive of their needs.

Set up the location of your study so everyone will be comfortable and feel like part of the group. Also, set up to play soft music during the reflection time.

Print handouts if needed.

Group Study

Introduction

Welcome all the girls as they come in and note any new attendees. If needed, make introductions once everyone is seated.

Pray

Invite the Holy Spirit to guide your discussion and open your hearts to His truth.

Review

Ask if anyone was able to make any changes in their media (or other) choices over the past week. If so, ask them if they would be willing to share something they changed.

Ask if any of the girls found changing media habits to be hard, and what kind of struggles they faced.

Ask if anyone wants to share something they read about from the past two chapters and how it impacted them.

Discuss

Pass out handouts or have girls flip to the questions in the back of their books, then discuss the questions.

1. What does Shelley's mom call the lies we believe? Do you think that's a good representation of those lies?

2. How can we replace the lies we believe with God's truth? What were the steps shared for weeding out lies in chapter six? *Leader's note: Have the girls flip there and make sure to cover the whole list.*

3. How can we know if we are putting too much stock into our outer beauty? *Leader's note: Ask the girls if they think they could go a whole day without makeup or looking into a mirror.*

4. Have you believed the lie that if you could change one thing about your body, that others would accept you and you would be able to accept yourself? Do you recognize it as a lie, or do you believe it's true?

5. Which of the stories shared in the book so far can you relate to the most? It could be a story from Amber, Rehan, Kandace, or one of the stories Shelley or Heather have shared.

Reflection

Ask the girls if they focus more on the weeds and/or "cracks on the floor" of their life than they do on God's truth. Consider sharing your own answer to this question.

Spend some quiet time and ask the girls to make a list in their journals (or on a sheet of paper) of all the lies they can think of that they have been believing. If you have enough time, you could also have them try to find a scripture to replace the lie with God's truth.

Prayer Time

Ask if the girls have any prayer requests. Close in prayer, mentioning any requests they had and praying for God to help open their eyes in the area of beauty and help them to see themselves the way that He sees them.

Before You Dismiss

Remind girls when your next meeting is and that they should:
- Finish their journal entry if they haven't already.
- Read chapters 8, 9 & 10 before the next session.

Also, remind the girls that you are available to talk with them one on one if needed.

Session Four

What Do You Believe?
Chapters 8, 9 & 10

Leader Preparation

Pray that God would help you to be content with the girls who show up. No matter who is there or not there, whether the number is big or small, ask that He equips you to be the leader they need and perceptive of their needs.

Set up the location of your study so everyone will be comfortable and feel like part of the group. Also, set up to play soft music during the reflection time.

Print handouts if needed.

Group Study

Introduction

Welcome all the girls as they come in and note any new attendees. If needed, make introductions once everyone is seated.

Pray

Invite the Holy Spirit to guide your discussion and open your hearts to His truth.

Review

Ask if anyone was able to do something this week to focus more on their inner beauty than on their outer beauty.

Ask if anyone wants to share something they read about from the three chapters they read for this session.

Discuss

Pass out handouts or have girls flip to the questions in the back of their books, then discuss the questions.

1. Did you ever consider that your beliefs about evolution and creationism could affect the way you view yourself and others? Why or why not?

2. What are some things we can know about ourselves based off the knowledge that we were created by God?

3. How can the way we view our earthly father affect the way we view our heavenly Father? Have you ever struggled with this?

4. Have you ever struggled with believing God's Word or understanding how it could be relevant to your life? Why or why not?

5. What are some ways we can know what God wants from us in modern-day dilemmas? Can you share an example?

6. *Have someone read 2 Timothy 3:16-17 aloud.* Based off that Scripture, how important is God's Word when it comes to being a Christian?

Reflection/ Prayer Time

Turn on some soft music, dim the lights and ask girls to bow their heads. With heads bowed and eyes closed, ask them to raise their hand if the following sentences can describe them at any point in their lives. (You may need to let them know to put their hand down after each sentence.)

- I have believed we evolved from nothing. That there was no creator and that I didn't matter in the grand scheme of things.

- I have felt like my life had no meaning.

- I have felt like I have no real beauty.

- I have felt alone, like no one really cares about me.

- I have compared God, our heavenly Father to my earthly Father.

- I have struggled to believe the Bible is true.

- I have had blind faith in the Bible.

- I have thought the Bible couldn't possibly be relevant to my life.

- I have set my Bible aside, and am trying to be a Christian without it.

Go straight in to prayer time. Pray for the lies you have been believing and that God would reach into the hearts of each girl in the room and show them the truth about Him, His Word, and His love for them.

Optional: After your prayer, ask girls (with eyes still closed) to stand up if they raised their hand for at least one question. Then have them open their eyes and look around. Remind them that they are not alone.

Before You Dismiss

Remind girls when your next meeting is and that they should:
- Read the reflection question on their own.
- Journal about one of the topics that they struggled with most from this week.
- Read chapters 11 & 12 before the next session.

Also, remind the girls that you are available to talk with them one on one if needed.

Session Five

Faith & Fashion
Chapters 11 & 12

Leader Preparation

Pray that God would help you to be content with the girls who show up. No matter who is there or not there, whether the number is big or small, ask that He equips you to be the leader they need and perceptive of their needs.

Set up the location of your study so everyone will be comfortable and feel like part of the group.

Print handouts if needed.

Print and cut out Beauty Cards (or make your own) for the activity in this session. Find out more at beautycards.TrueBeautyBook.com

Group Study

Introduction

Welcome all the girls as they come in and note any new attendees. If needed, make introductions once everyone is seated.

Pray

Invite the Holy Spirit to guide your discussion and open your hearts to His truth.

Review

Ask if everyone was able to read the last two chapters and if anyone wants to share something they read.

Discuss

Pass out handouts or have girls flip to the questions in the back of their books, then discuss the questions.

1. *Have girls flip to chapter 11 and ask them to read the four ways we publicize ourselves.* Based on those points, do you think others see you the way you really want them to?

2. What do you think plays into the way guys treat girls? Does our clothing matter? Why or why not?

3. What would you say influences you the most in regards to the clothes you buy and wear?

4. In chapter 12, Shelley shared four things she discovered about her clothing choices. Can you relate to any of them, or see how they might be true in your life?

5. *Have someone read Luke 17:1-3 and someone else read Matthew 5:28, then discuss* how can those verses relate to the way we dress. Do you think we have a responsibility in helping the guys around us to have pure thoughts?

Activity

Have the girls divide into two (or more) groups. Give each group a set of "Beauty Cards" but don't let them look at them. Tell the groups that each set of cards contains different ideas about how we can invest in our beauty. They need to divide the cards into two groups, inner beauty or outer beauty. Then, they have to come up with one more way they can invest in their inner beauty. The first group to finish, wins. Give them a count down, and have each group start at the same time. "Ready? 3, 2, 1, go!"

After the activity is over, have each group share the idea they came up with for investing in their inner beauty.

Prayer Time

Ask if the girls have any prayer requests. Close in prayer, mentioning any requests they had and praying for God to help open their eyes in the area of beauty and help them to see themselves the way that He sees them.

Before You Dismiss

Remind girls when your next meeting is and that they should:
- Read the reflection question and complete the journal entry.
- Read chapters 13 & 14 before the next session.
- Ask them to where an outfit they think is both trendy and modest to the next session.

And remind them that you are available to talk with them if needed.

Session Six
Modest is Hottest
Chapters 13 & 14

Leader Preparation

Pray that God would help you to be content with the girls who show up. No matter who is there or not there, whether the number is big or small, ask that He equips you to be the leader they need and perceptive of their needs.

Set up the location of your study so everyone will be comfortable and feel like part of the group.

Print handouts if needed.

Consider wearing your own modest, yet trendy, outfit.

Supplies
- Sticky notes
- Markers

Group Study

Introduction

Welcome all the girls as they come in and comment on their outfits.

Pray

Invite the Holy Spirit to guide your discussion, open your hearts to His truth, and help you to have fun together, but still keep Him in mind.

Review

Let the girls know that you are halfway through the study, and ask if any of them wants to share the biggest way this study has impacted them so far.

Ask if everyone had a chance to read the chapters for this week and if anyone wants to share something they read.

Discuss

Pass out handouts or have girls flip to the questions in the back of their books, then discuss the questions.

1. Is it possible to dress trendy, but not trashy? To be both modern and modest?

2. Are there any "Modesty Tips" that Shelley shared that you feel God would like you to work on? What solutions could you try?

3. How about swimwear? Do you think God cares about what we wear swimming?

4. Assign the following verses to different girls and have them read them aloud: 1 Corinthians 6:19-20, Ephesians 5:3, Matthew 5:28, and Luke 17:1-3 (you can look them up in your Bible, or in chapter 14 in your book). Discuss how those verses relate to what we wear.

5. Why do you think it's important to dress modestly? Where does modesty start?

6. Do you have a gift or talent that displays your inner beauty?

Fashion Show

Have each of the girls display their modest, but trendy outfit. Have the other girls comment on what they like about it. Either have girls volunteer to come up front, or make sure everyone gets a turn. If you want, pair girls into groups of two and have them announce each other's outfits. Have them note what's trendy and what's modest.

Afterwards, divide the girls into 2-3 groups. (If there's not enough they can all work together.) Have them get in a circle with their group and place several pretty colored post-it notes on the floor in the middle. Make sure everyone has a marker to write with. Tell them that they are preparing for "God's beauty pageant".

Their job is to choose one person to be the model and then have everyone in their group (model can do this too) write characteristics on the post-it notes that they think God would consider beautiful and use them to "dress" the model!! Encourage them to write both inner qualities and also outer appearance qualities (such as how they dress, talk, act, etc.) They also need to choose a different person to be the "spokeswoman" and "announce" what the model is wearing as they "come down the runway"!! Take turns having each group share and applaud after each one.

After both fashion shows, ask the girls if they think dressing modestly can be fun and trendy. Encourage them to keep thinking of ways they can honor God with the way the dress each day.

Prayer Time

Ask if the girls have any prayer requests. Close in prayer, mentioning any requests they had and thanking God for allowing us to have fun while still honoring Him and His Word.

Before You Dismiss

Remind girls when your next meeting is and that they should:
- Read the reflection question and complete their journal entry.
- Read chapters 15 & 16 before the next session.

Session Seven

Boy Crazy
Chapters 15 & 16

Leader Preparation

Pray that God would help you to be content with the girls who show up. No matter who is there or not there, whether the number is big or small, ask that He equips you to be the leader they need and perceptive of their needs.

Set up the location of your study so everyone will be comfortable and feel like part of the group.

Print handouts if needed.

Group Study

Introduction

Welcome all the girls as they come in, commenting on any trendy and modest outfits.

Pray

Invite the Holy Spirit to guide your discussion and open your hearts to His truth.

Review

Ask if any of the girls spent more time creating trendy modest outfits. Then ask if anyone invested in their inner beauty.

Ask if they had a chance to read the chapters for today's session and if they have anything they want to share before you begin.

Discuss

Pass out handouts or have girls flip to the questions in the back of their books, then discuss the questions.

1. Do you believe that flirting is just innocent fun, or do you see how it could be dangerous?

2. What advice or instruction have you had in the area of sex and dating, and who did it come from?

3. *Ask someone to read Song of Songs 2:7 aloud.* What are some ways we might "arouse or awaken love?"

4. What are some characteristics of the love God wants us to share with others? *If you're not getting answers, ask the*

girls to open their Bibles to 1 Corinthians 13 and look at verses 4-8 and see what is says.

5. Do you see how Heather easily got caught up in the fun vs. forever mindset? How can we avoid that in our own lives?

Reflection

Ask the girls to write down something they would like to do, that they might not be able to if they had a boyfriend. Have them add to their list things they do in their free time that they might not have time for if they were dating.

Go around the room and have each girl share one thing from her list.

Optional: Play the song, "Wait for Me" by Rebecca St. James as they write.

Prayer Time

Ask if the girls have any prayer requests. Close in prayer, mentioning any requests they had and praying for God to help each of them value the gift of singleness. Also ask that God would help them to love all people the way He loves them.

Before You Dismiss

Remind girls when your next meeting is and that they should:
- Read the reflection question and complete their journal entry.
- Read chapters 17 & 18 before the next session.

Also remind them that you are available to talk with them if needed.

Session Eight

Guys vs. Girls
Chapters 17 & 18

Leader Preparation

Pray that God would help you to be content with the girls who show up. No matter who is there or not there, whether the number is big or small, ask that He equips you to be the leader they need and perceptive of their needs.

Set up the location of your study so everyone will be comfortable and feel like part of the group.

Print handouts if needed.

Supplies
- Whiteboard
- Duct tape

Group Study

Introduction

Welcome all the girls as they come in and note any new attendees. If needed, make introductions.

Pray

Invite the Holy Spirit to guide your discussion and open your hearts to His truth.

Opening Activity

Ask someone to write on a dry erase board. At the top of the board write, "Emotions we might feel…" and then make 2 columns, "While dating someone" and "After a break up". Have the girls take turns sharing an emotion and which column they would put it under.

Discuss

Pass out handouts or have girls flip to the questions in the back of their books, then discuss the questions.

1. Have you ever felt depressed after a break up? If so, why do you think you felt that why?

2. What are some ways we can guard our hearts in relationships?

3. What are some consequences of not keeping the "fire" of our sexual passion inside the "fireplace" of marriage?

4. What are some practical ways you can honor God when it comes it romance and dating? How can you protect your purity and reserve intimacy for marriage?

5. *Have someone read Ephesians 6:10-18 where it talks about the armor of God.* How can those verses help us keep from going too far with guys?

Activity

Take a strip of duct tape and tape it to your arm (on the side with hair). Make sure it's on good and tight, then peel it off.

Now, pass that strip of duct tape to the girl that's closest to you and have her do the same. Then pass it to the next girl and have her repeat the process passing it on until it simply won't stick any more. Note after each girl peels it off if any hair or skin was left behind (and if anyone else's hair is still attached).

Once it stops sticking, ask the girl who is left holding the duct tape if she wants to keep it. Ask the group as a whole if they needed to hold something together, if they would want that piece of duct tape, or a new one.

Ask the girls if they remember this example from the book. Then ask if they can see how the bond weakens over time. Encourage them that unlike the duct tape, if they have already gone too far, it's not too late for them. Let them know that God can give them their "sticky" back. That when they truly regret what they have done and are willing to repent, that God can make them new. He can restore them in a way nothing else can.

Prayer Time

Close in prayer asking God to guard the hearts of the girls in your group. Ask Him to help keep them pure and restore the purity of those who may have already lost it, helping them to stay pure from today forward.

Before You Dismiss

Remind girls when your next meeting is and that they should:
- Read and think about the reflection question.
- Complete the journal entry.
- Read chapters 19, 20 & 21 before the next session.

Remind the girls that you are covering some pretty tough topics and that you are available to talk with them if needed. You can also let them know they can go visit FindYourTrueBeauty.com and reach out to Heather if they aren't comfortable sharing with you or want to remain anonymous.

Session Nine
When Sex Isn't Sexy
Chapters 19, 20 & 21

Leader Preparation

Pray that God would help you to be content with the girls who show up. No matter who is there or not there, whether the number is big or small, ask that He equips you to be the leader they need and perceptive of their needs.

Set up the location of your study so everyone will be comfortable and feel like part of the group.

Print handouts if needed.

Supplies
- Note cards
- Blindfolds

Group Study

Introduction

Welcome all the girls as they come in and let them know you are glad they came.

Prayer Activity

Pass out note cards to all the girls. Have each of them write down any prayer requests that are related to the topics you will be covering today (the link between sex and depression, sexual abuse, and homosexuality). Their requests could be for themselves or for someone they know who might be struggling with one of those topics. If they don't want to name names, let them know they can just write that they have a friend who struggles with _____ or even just write down the topic they are thinking of.

Once they are finished, collect the cards and, without looking at them, pray for God to reach into each situation that is listed. For the girls in your study, for their friends, for their families, for anyone who could possibly be involved. Ask Him to give them comfort and healing and for Him to be your guide as you study these tough topics.

Discuss

Pass out handouts or have girls flip to the questions in the back of their books, then discuss the questions.

1. Do you see how there can be a link between sex and depression?

2. Would you know if you were sexually abused? Did any of the definitions of sexual abuse surprise you?

3. *Have someone read James 1:4-5 aloud and then discuss the process of sin.* Is it the temptation that's wrong? If you are willing, share how you have seen this process work in your life.

4. Is it hard for you to believe that God loves everyone, including drug addicts, murders, homosexuals, cheaters, anorexics, etc.? Why or why not?

5. How does God's view of homosexuality differ from that of the culture?

6. How do you think God wants us to respond to homosexuals?

Activity

Divide the group in half. Give half of the girls blindfolds and make sure they are secured. After they are blindfolded, have the other half of the girls silently choose a blindfolded partner. Let the girls know that their blindfolded partner should not know who they are. It's a secret.

Then, have the girls who are not blindfolded lead their partners around the room. They can hold their arm to guide them, only the blindfolded person may talk - the guide must stay silent. If you set up a course ahead of time, have them use it now.

At the end of the walk, have each guide return their blindfolded partner to where they started and then walk back to where their group started. The blindfolded girls can then remove the blindfolds. Ask them to guess who guided them around the room.

Ask the girls if it was important for them to know who was guiding them (and why or why not). Ask them if they think it's important for them to know who or what is guiding their choices when it comes to real life.

(This activity is based off of an activity found in the Ghost Ranch Ropes Course Manual, by Dr. Sylvia Shirley.)

Prayer Time

Ask if the girls have any prayer requests. Close in prayer, mentioning any requests they had and praying for God to be your guide both in the coming week and beyond.

Before You Dismiss

Remind girls when your next meeting is and that they should:
- Read the reflection question and complete their journal entry.
- Read chapters 22 & 23 before the next session.

Remind the girls that you are covering some pretty tough topics and that you are available to talk with them if needed. You can also let them know they can go visit FindYourTrueBeauty.com and reach out to Heather if they aren't comfortable sharing with you or want to remain anonymous.

Session Ten
Find Your True Beauty
Chapters 22 & 23

Leader Preparation

Pray that God would help you to be content with the girls who show up. No matter who is there or not there, whether the number is big or small, ask that He equips you to be the leader they need and perceptive of their needs.

Set up the location of your study so everyone will be comfortable and feel like part of the group. For today's activity, use masking tape to tape two lines (or trails) on the floor. They should not be straight. They can be as long or as short as you like, but make sure they have at least two turns.

Print handouts if needed.

Supplies
- Masking tape
- Blindfolds

Group Study

Introduction

Welcome all the girls as they come in and note any new attendees. If needed, make introductions.

Pray

Invite the Holy Spirit to guide your discussion and open your hearts to His truth.

Review

Ask if anyone wants to share something they read about from the two chapters for this week and how it impacted them.

Discuss

Pass out handouts or have girls flip to the questions in the back of their books, then discuss the questions.

1. When do you feel closest to God?

2. What are some of the things we choose to do instead of connecting with God?

3. Do you see the importance when it comes to spending time with God every day?

4. *Have someone read Psalm 42:1-2 aloud.* Do you thirst for God? If not, what might be the cause?

5. What are some examples of wrong paths we can go down in life? Paths that might not seem bad, but won't lead us toward becoming godly women with true beauty?

6. At the end of Julie's story, she discovered that we are all different, and that's the way God intended us to be. How are you different? Do you see your difference as a bad thing, or have you accepted it as God's design?

Reflection

Divide girls into two teams and ask each team to select a volunteer. Then have the teams blindfold their volunteer and guide them to the start of one of the two lines you made earlier. Once on the line, both teams should use vocal cues to guide their teammate to the other end of the line. (This will be difficult with everyone talking at once – let it play out.) First person to the finish line wins, but have the blindfolded girls leave their blindfolds on.

Ask the girls who are blindfolded if it was easy or hard to stay on their course, and why.

Now, have the teams take turns calling their teammate by name and guiding them back to the starting point. (e.g., Team A: "Alison, take one step forward." Team B: "Brittney, turn to the right." Team A: "Alison, take a step to the left." Team B: … etc.")

Once the girls get back to the starting point ask them if it was easier that time and why.

Ask if any of the girls can figure out how the activity relates to today's session.

The relation is that while we are going through our daily lives, we have lots of different voices pulling us in different directions and it's easy to get off course. But, when we listen for God's voice, it's easier to stay on track.

Variation

If you are short on time, make one line instead of two. Select two volunteers, one will be the blindfolded traveler, and the other will be their guide. Once the blindfolded traveler is on the start of the line, have everyone start giving random directions. Have the other volunteer call her by name and guide her down the line.

Once she reaches the end, ask her how she was able to get there.

Answer: by listening to the right voice.

Prayer Time

Ask if the girls have any prayer requests. Close in prayer, mentioning any requests they had and praying for God to help open their eyes in the area of beauty and help them to see themselves the way that He sees them.

Before You Dismiss

Remind girls when your next meeting is and that they should:
- Read the reflection question and complete their journal entry.
- Read chapters 24 & 25 before the next session.
- Also, ask girls to bring their security blanket, or a favorite animal from when you were younger to the next session.

And, as always, remind them that you are available to talk if needed.

Session Eleven
The Beauty of Hope
Chapters 24 & 25

Leader Preparation

Pray that God would help you to be content with the girls who show up. No matter who is there or not there, whether the number is big or small, ask that He equips you to be the leader they need and perceptive of their needs.

Before the lesson, take the time to cut out enough paper hearts for each girl to have one. Tear each heart in half to represent a "broken heart". Also, print and cut out several copies of Psalm 147:3 and make sure the hearts are big enough for you to tape a verse to each one once it's been taped back together.

Set up the location of your study so everyone will be comfortable and feel like part of the group.

Print handouts if needed.

Consider bringing your own security item or the item from one of your children.

Supplies
- Construction paper (for hearts)
- Tape

Group Study

Introduction

Welcome all the girls as they come in.

Pray

Invite the Holy Spirit to guide your discussion and open your hearts to His truth.

Review

Ask if anyone wants to share something they read about from the past two chapters and how it impacted them.

Discuss

Pass out handouts or have girls flip to the questions in the back of their books, then discuss the questions.

1. Have you ever felt brokenhearted? *Go around the room and have each of the girls say one word describing the cause of their broken heart. You can start off, here are some examples: divorce, breakup, loneliness, rejection, abuse, etc.*

2. In chapter 24, Shelley mentioned five things that helped her heal her broken heart, what were they? *(See the section titled "What Helped Me.")*

3. What are the three parts of the forgiveness cross?

4. *Have someone read Ephesians 4:31 aloud and then identify the six things God wants us to get rid of as a group. Then, discuss how unforgiveness can cause those things.*

5. *Have each girl share a memory they have about the security blanket, animal, or item they brought today. If they didn't bring one, but still have a memory they can share, encourage them to do so.*

Do you believe that God loves you more than you used to love that toy or blanket? That there is nothing you could do and nothing could be done to you that would ever change His love for you? Why or why not?

Activity & Prayer

Place enough "torn hearts" around on the table for each girl to have one. Explain to the girls that they are to choose two halves that make up one heart and place them in front of them. Ask them to then close their eyes. Let them know that you are going to come around and tape their heart back together. Encourage them as their eyes are closed to try and imagine Jesus coming alongside them and stitching their heart back together. They can use this quiet time to pray and ask God to heal their own heart if it is broken, or if they are not struggling with a broken heart, they can thank God for a time He helped them or pray for someone else they know who has a broken heart.

Go around and tape up each heart one at a time and also tape the verse, Psalm 147:3 on each heart.

When you finish taping up all of the hearts, say a prayer of thanks to God for the healing He offers us in Christ.

Ask if anyone would like to share some things that helped them to heal when they had a broken heart? *(Leaders: Feel free to share a personal story if you feel it would benefit the girls.)*

End by having someone read Psalm 34:18.

Before You Dismiss

Remind girls when your next meeting is and that they should:
- Read the reflection question and complete their journal entry.
- Read chapter 26 before the next session. Also encourage them to read the appendix if they haven't already.

Also, remind them that you are still available to talk with them if needed.

Session Twelve

You Are Beautiful
Chapter 26

Leader Preparation

Pray that God would help you to be content with the girls who show up. No matter who is there or not there, whether the number is big or small, ask that He equips you to be the leader they need and perceptive of their needs.

Set up the location of your study so everyone will be comfortable and feel like part of the group.

Print handouts if needed.

Group Study

Introduction

Welcome all the girls to the last session as they come in.

Pray

Thank God for all He has been teaching you through this study and ask Him to guide your final time together.

Discuss

Pass out handouts or have girls flip to the questions in the back of their books, then discuss the questions.

1. How does the world define beauty? What are some of the ways believing the world's definition of beauty can influence us or harm us?

2. How does God define beauty? What does knowing God's definition of beauty teach us?

3. Looking back over this book, what is one thing that has surprised, influenced, or helped you the most?

4. In what ways could you relate to the "Who Am I" poem at the end of the book?

5. Read Romans 12:2 and discuss how you can transform your mind when it comes to beauty.

Reflection

Have girls write their own "Who Am I" poem to share with the group. Give them 5-10 minutes to write, and then have each of them read it aloud.

Prayer Time

Ask if the girls have any prayer requests. Close in prayer, mentioning any requests they had and praying for God to help open their eyes in the area of beauty and help them to see themselves the way that He sees them.

Before You Dismiss

Remind them that even though the study is over, they can still talk with you if they want to.

If you are planning on doing another study, let them know what it is and when it will start. You can see our list of recommended studies at the back of this book.

Dear Leader,

Thank you for doing this study! You have been a vessel that God has used to speak His truth into these girls' lives! Remember the words spoken in Isaiah 55:10-11, *"As the rain and the snow come down from heaven, and do not return to it without watering the earth and making it bud and flourish, so that it yields seed for the sower and bread for the eater, so is my word that goes out from my mouth. It will not return to me empty, but will accomplish what I desire and achieve the purpose for which I sent it."*

Your sisters in Christ,
Shelley and Heather

P.S. If you have found this guide helpful for leading your group of girls through this study, would you mind taking a minute to write a review on Amazon to let other leaders know?

About the Authors

Shelley Hitz is an award-winning and international best-selling author. However, most importantly she is a wife, daughter, sister, friend and follower of Christ. She has a heart for teen girls that began from her own journey of finding her true beauty in Christ. Shelley is currently ministering to Christian entrepreneurs (pastors, authors, speakers, business owners) who want to keep Christ at the center of their lives and business.

Heather Hart is first and foremost a servant of Christ who is happily married to the man of her dreams—but she's also the mother of four, an internationally best-selling and award-winning author, and the director of FindYourTrueBeauty.com. She doesn't have it all together, but she's okay with that because she knows Christ has her covered when she fails. Her hope that is while she is struggling through this thing called life, she is pointing others towards Jesus along the way.

Contact Information

We would love to hear from you! Send us an email or a letter to one of the following addresses:

Heather Hart
P.O. Box 1277
Seymour, TX 76380

Shelley Hitz
P.O. Box 6542
Colorado Springs, CO 80934

heather@teen-beauty-tips.com
shelley@shelleyhitz.com

Or visit our website at
www.findyourtruebeauty.com

Prayer Requests: Send in your prayer requests, so we can pray specifically for you at http://Prayer.TrueBeautyBook.com

Recommended Bible Studies for Teen Girls

Seemless
Understanding the Bible as One Complete Story
by Angie Smith

Girl Defined
God's Radical Design for Beauty, Femininity, and Identity
by Kristen Clark and Bethany Baird

Wonderfully Made
Becoming Who You Are In Christ
by Allie Marie Smith

Lies Young Women Believe
And the Truth that Sets Them Free
by Nancy Leigh DeMoss and Danna Gresh

Find more our complete list of recommended studies at
Recommended.TrueBeautyBook.com

Made in the USA
Lexington, KY
03 June 2018